THANK YOU,
SHARKS

BY MARTY ERICKSON

The Child's World®
childsworld.com

Published by The Child's World®
1980 Lookout Drive • Mankato, MN 56003-1705
800-599-READ • www.childsworld.com

Photographs ©: Natalia Tamkovich/Shutterstock Images, cover, 1; Krzysztof Odziomek/Shutterstock Images, 2, 9; Tomas Kotouc/Shutterstock Images, 5; Gab Riel/Shutterstock Images, 6; Frantise Khojdysz/Shutterstock Images, 10, 24; SkyPics Studio/Shutterstock Images, 13 (shark); Shutterstock Images, 13 (large fish), 13 (squid), 13 (plant), 13 (small fish), 13 (shrimp); Izen Kai/Shutterstock Images, 14; Andrea Izzotti/Shutterstock Images, 17; Julian Gunther/Shutterstock Images, 18; Stefan Pircher/Shutterstock Images, 21

ISBN 9781503850088 (Reinforced Library Binding)
ISBN 9781503850521 (Portable Document Format)
ISBN 9781503851283 (Online Multi-user eBook)
LCCN 2021939910

Printed in the United States of America

ABOUT THE AUTHOR

Marty Erickson is a writer living in Minnesota. They write books for young people full time and like to go hiking.

TABLE OF CONTENTS

CHAPTER ONE

Ruler of the Oceans

A whitetip **reef** shark swims in the warm water. The coral reef is full of colorful fish. Starfish cling to rocks. The shark cruises through the reef's narrow channels. It has a skinny, gray body. The shark can make tight turns.

Sunlight shines on the water's surface. Light ripples through the water. Soon, four more whitetip reef sharks arrive. It is not time to hunt yet. The sharks wait for the sun to set.

Whitetip reef sharks hunt in packs at night.

Whitetip reef sharks have narrow bodies. This allows them to hunt fish that are hiding in tight places.

In the dark, the sharks look for **prey**. Fish dart into holes. Others swim away from the sharks. One shark sees a fish swimming alone. It is easy to catch. The shark bites the fish. Some of the other sharks swim over. They each try to take a bite of the fish.

Sharks live in oceans around the world. There are more than 440 types of sharks. The smallest shark is only 8 inches (20 cm) long. The largest shark is bigger than a school bus. Some sharks live in cold water. Others prefer warm, shallow water.

Sharks **adapted** to the places in which they live. Some sharks swim fast to catch prey. Other sharks swim slowly and eat small animals on the ocean floor. Sharks are an important part of their **habitats**. They eat other animals. They keep their habitats balanced.

FUN FACT

The Greenland shark can live up to 400 years!

Whale sharks are the largest sharks on Earth. They can grow to be 59 feet (18 m) long.

Scientists believe hammerhead sharks have been swimming the oceans for 35 to 50 million years.

Oceans in Balance

Sharks have been around for millions of years. Scientists study shark **fossils**. These fossils show scientists that sharks were alive at the same time as dinosaurs.

Oceans have many types of plants and animals. A healthy ocean has the right balance of many types of creatures. Everything is connected. Sharks play a role in this.

Scientists know plants and animals are connected. Animals are also connected to other animals. Scientists use food webs. Food webs show how animals and plants need one another. Food webs also show how animals need other animals.

Small fish eat seagrass. Bigger fish eat the small fish. Sharks often eat the larger animals. Sharks are **predators**. They have sharp teeth to grab prey.

FUN FACT

Some sharks may lose 35,000 teeth in their lifetimes.

Ocean Food Web

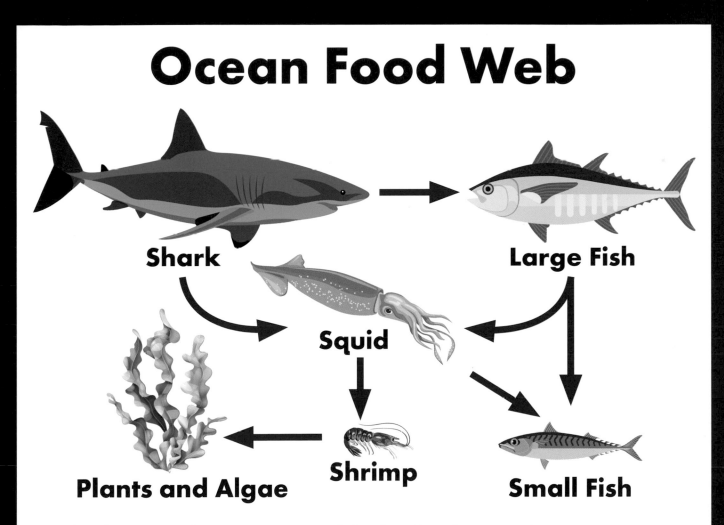

Shark

Large Fish

Squid

Plants and Algae

Shrimp

Small Fish

Sharks are an important part of the food web. By eating some animals, they help protect others.

Sharks eat many different types of animals.

Some sharks eat other animals such as turtles, mammals, or **crustaceans**. They keep the number of bigger fish down. This protects the small animals and plants.

But sharks also feed the smallest animals. Sharks' bodies sink to the ocean floor when they die. Small animals eat the sharks' bodies. A large shark can feed many animals. Without sharks, there would be less food for animals on the ocean floor.

CHAPTER THREE

Life without Sharks

Sharks face many threats. Some people fish for sharks on purpose. People around the world eat shark meat. Some people are afraid of sharks. They want to get rid of these animals.

Other people kill sharks by accident. Sharks may get caught in fishing nets. Some types of sharks cannot breathe if they stop swimming. These sharks die in fishing nets.

People are the biggest threat to sharks. Many sharks are killed by people fishing.

Baby sharks are called pups.

It is important to protect sharks. Sharks grow slowly. It takes many years before a shark is an adult.

Some kinds of sharks do not have many babies at once. This makes it difficult for these shark **populations** to grow. Without sharks, many other plants and animals are affected.

FUN FACT

Some sharks give birth to live pups. Other sharks lay eggs.

When sharks leave an area, fish populations grow. When there are too many small fish, they will eat too many ocean plants. Eventually ocean grasses do not grow back.

Similarly, when there are too many large fish, they will eat too many of the small ocean animals. When this happens, habitats have fewer types of plants and animals. Oceans are not as healthy. Sharks play an important part in their environment. They are predators. Sharks keep oceans healthy.

Many countries, such as the United States and Mexico, have passed laws to help protect sharks.

GLOSSARY

adapted (uh-DAP-tehd) Adapted means to have changed in order to survive in a place. Sharks adapted to live in different parts of the ocean.

crustaceans (kruss-TAY-shunz) Crustaceans are animals that have hard bodies and two pairs of antennae. Shrimp, crabs, and lobsters are all crustaceans.

fossils (FAHSS-uhls) Fossils are the remains of plants and animals that lived at least 10,000 years ago. Scientists study shark fossils.

habitats (HA-buh-tats) Habitats are places with the right temperature, weather, food, and water for an animal to live. Ocean habitats have many types of animals.

populations (pop-yoo-LAY-shunz) Populations are the numbers of animals in a certain area. Overfishing hurts shark populations.

predators (PREH-duh-tuhrs) Predators are animals that hunt and eat other animals. Sharks are predators.

prey (PRAY) Prey are animals that are eaten by predators. The shark catches prey with its sharp teeth.

reef (REEF) A reef is a shallow area in the ocean with many types of plants and animals. A shark looks for food in a reef.

TO LEARN MORE

BOOKS

Koestler-Grack, Rachel. *10 Fascinating Facts about Sharks*. New York, NY: Children's Press, 2017.

Laughlin, Kara L. *Sharks*. Mankato, MN: The Child's World, 2017.

Williams, Lily. *If Sharks Disappeared*. New York, NY: Roaring Brook, 2017.

WEBSITES

Visit our website for links about sharks:
childsworld.com/links

Note to Parents, Teachers, and Librarians: We routinely verify our Web links to make sure they are safe and active sites. So encourage your readers to check them out!

INDEX